THE DOMINIE WORLD OF ANIMALS

# POLAR BEARS

Graham Meadows & Claire Vial

## Contents

DOMINIE PRESS

Pearson Learning Group

## *About Polar Bears*

Polar bears are the world's largest land **carnivores** and the largest members of the bear family.

Their **habitat** covers the vast, **frigid** polar regions surrounding the Arctic Circle. They are found in Norway, Russia, Canada, Greenland, and the state of Alaska.

Polar bears are generally **solitary** animals, except for females with their babies.

Male polar bears are called boars. Females are called sows. Babies are called cubs.

## *Where Polar Bears Live*

Polar bears range over large areas called **home ranges**. They live mostly on the shorelines and sea ice. They use sea ice as a platform for hunting seals. Because large areas of sea ice melt in summer and form again in winter, polar bears must be constantly on the move.

It is very cold in the world of snow and ice where polar bears live. In winter the air temperature can fall to forty or fifty degrees below zero (Fahrenheit).

On very cold days when the wind is very strong, polar bears dig a temporary shelter in the snow and curl themselves up into a ball.

## *Their Shape and Size*

Male polar bears weigh between 750 and 1,400 pounds. Most males are a little over five feet high at the shoulders, and about nine feet long from nose to tail. Female polar bears are much smaller and lighter. They weigh between 330 and 550 pounds, and are about seven feet long.

The largest polar bear ever recorded was twelve feet long and weighed 2,200 pounds.

## *Their Skin*

Polar bears' skin is black. Their skin helps to keep them warm because black absorbs more heat from the sun than any other color. Glands in their skin produce oil that spreads through the coat and helps to keep it waterproof.

Beneath the skin there is an insulating layer of fat, about four inches thick, that helps to keep the bears warm. The fat also helps to keep them afloat when they are swimming.

Polar bears are so well-insulated that they sometimes feel too warm. When this happens, they sprawl out on the ice to cool down.

## *Their Coats*

Polar bears have thick coats with two layers of hair, an undercoat and a topcoat. The dense, wooly undercoat is made of fine, white hairs. The hairs in the topcoat are coarse, hollow, and transparent. The hollow hairs keep the polar bears warm and help them to float in the water.

Polar bear coats range in color from creamy yellow to light brown. Their fur looks white because it reflects light from the snow. This helps to **camouflage** them when they are hunting their **prey**.

## How They Swim

Polar bears are very good swimmers. They can swim at about six miles an hour and up to sixty miles between ice floes. They paddle with their very large front paws, which are about one foot wide. Each front paw has small webs of skin between the toes, which help the polar bears to swim.

Polar bears often swim ten to fourteen feet below the water's surface.

A polar bear can stay under water and hold its breath for more than two minutes.

## *How Polar Bears Walk*

Polar bears walk on the soles of their feet, with their heels touching the ground first. Fur between their footpads helps them to grip the ice when they are walking or running. This fur also helps them to move quietly when they **stalk** their prey.

Polar bears usually walk very slowly, and they stop frequently to rest. If they move too quickly, they become too hot.

If necessary, polar bears can run faster than twenty-five miles an hour over short distances.

## *How They Hunt*

Ringed seals are polar bear's main prey. In early summer, the polar bears stalk seals that are lying on the sea ice or swimming in the water.

During winter, the bears wait very quietly by holes in the ice where the seals come up to breathe. When the seals come up for air, the polar bears knock them out with their paws or grab them in their powerful jaws and pull them out of the water.

A polar bear can lift a 550-pound seal in its jaws.

## *Their Diet*

In summer, much of the sea ice melts and breaks up. This is when it is more difficult for polar bears to catch seals. During this time, the bears look for other food. Their **diet** can include seabirds and their eggs, reindeer, walruses, caribou, and the remains of dead animals. Polar bears also **graze** on grass and seaweed, eat berries, and dig into the ground to eat the roots of plants.

Polar bears do not need to drink water because they get enough moisture from the food they eat.

## *Their Families*

Female polar bears usually **mate** when they are five to six years old, at the beginning of winter. They dig a **den** in the snow. About six weeks after they have entered the den, the females give birth, usually to two cubs.

At birth each cub weighs just over one pound. The cubs are deaf, blind, and completely helpless. They grow quickly as they **suckle** because a female polar bear's milk is rich in fat.

When spring arrives, the females and their cubs leave the den. By this time the cubs are about three months old and weigh about twenty-two pounds.

## How Young Polar Bears Grow Up

About two weeks after leaving the den, the female polar bear leads the cubs onto the sea ice. There the mother makes her first kill of the year and her cubs get their first taste of meat. The cubs continue to grow quickly on a high-fat diet of their mother's milk, seal meat, and blubber. By the time they are eight months old, the cubs weigh about 100 pounds.

Polar bear cubs learn to hunt by watching their mother. When they are two to three years old, they can **survive** on their own. From this time on, they start to lead a solitary life. They meet up with other polar bears only in order to mate and create the next generation of polar bears.

# Glossary

**camouflage:** A disguise that makes something blend in with its surroundings

**carnivores:** Animals that hunt, catch, and eat other animals

**den:** A safe place where a wild animal gives birth, takes shelter, rests, or sleeps

**diet:** The food that an animal or a person usually eats

**frigid:** Very, very cold

**graze:** To eat, or feed, on plants

**habitat:** A place where animals and plants live and grow

**home range:** The area over which an animal moves around and hunts

**mate:** To join with another animal in order to produce offspring

**prey:** Animals that are hunted and eaten by other animals

**solitary:** Without company; living alone

**stalk:** To follow, or track, an animal

**suckle:** To drink a mother's milk

**survive:** To stay alive

# Index